Confidence Is My Portion

30 Days of Affirmations to Renew
Your Sense of Self and Ignite a Bold,
New Self-Confidence Through Christ

By: Cynthia C. Farmer

Bonus Edition: 10-day Scripture-Led Journal
Confidence Is My Portion
30 Days of Affirmations to Renew Your Sense of
Self and Ignite a Bold, New Self-Confidence
Through Christ

Copyright © 2019 by Cynthia C. Farmer
Independently published

Bonus Edition

Unless otherwise noted, Scripture quotations are
taken from the King James Version.

Author Portrait by Louis Gilbert Photography. Used
by Permission.

ISBN: 9781798755327

Printed in the United States of America

Foreword

Life is real! But so is God! Yet, all too often, we find ourselves living and reacting physically to the things that are happening to us in the spiritual. We begin to believe the lies our situations tell us. We make promises to ourselves based on the lies of our emotions. Granted, our emotions are real, but they are based on the facts of our situations and not the truth. The more we use our physical energy to react, worry, stress, and the like, the more it begins to chip away at our self-confidence. At times, we put our everything into the things that are happening to us, and we still find ourselves failing. Whether it be an internal battle in our minds and hearts or the external battles of life, it all takes a toll on our confidence; we feel like we're losing or have lost the battle.

Truth be told, the only reason we lose these battles is because we are fighting the wrong way and not seeing God's truth. And when we fight the wrong way and fight blindly, we lose each and every time and our confidence takes a hit! So it's time to take a step in the right direction, rebuild our confidence through Christ, and get ready to fight the right way! It's time to operate in truth! It's time to win!

The number 3 in the Bible represents completeness, while 8 represents new beginnings. Often times, the battles we face in the physical can be become so daunting that we begin to lose confidence in Christ and in ourselves, and our focus shifts to our issues instead of remaining on God. It is important to remember that the battles we face are not physical battles but are spiritual battles that we must fight correctly (Ephesians 6:10). We must not become so dismayed that we remove our helmet of salvation, allowing the enemy to infiltrate our minds, shifting our focus from God to our problems and making them appear larger than life! But as we know, the devil is a lying, conniving, slithering creature. And although we should not take his tricks and tactics lightly, we ought to approach every battle with the posture of confidence because of the God we serve and the gift of His Holy Spirit within us. With the numbers 3 and 8 holding power, it is my prayer that the 30 affirmations in this devotional will give you just that – the power of true completion and a new beginning in Christ.

And the work of righteousness shall be peace; and the effect of righteousness quietness and assurance for ever. – Isaiah 32:17

Opening Prayer
(Read twice and sign when ready)

Dear Heavenly Father,

Most gracious, unchanging, unyielding, loving, merciful, awesome, comforting God, you are the way, the truth, and the life. You are a healer, a provider, a conqueror, and my God. I am your namesake, your heir, your daughter. I am a recipient of the kingdom you have created. All that you have done, all that you're doing, and all that you are going to do is for me! Who am I that you would choose to give your whole kingdom to me? Your word says, "For by grace [I] have been saved through faith. And this is not [my] own doing; it is the gift of God."

Father, I thank you for the gift of eternal life, unconditional love, and unwavering forgiveness. As I read this devotional and read your Word, may I be changed and made bold in my love for you and my love for myself through you. Refine me and purify me into every bit of the

Woman of God you have purposed me to be. Manifest in me the fruits of the Holy Spirit – joy, love, peace, longsuffering, gentleness, meekness, goodness, faith, and temperance. Remove from my heart, my mind, and my life any and everything that is not of you and was not sent by you.

Through you I am saved, I am whole, I am worthy, I am fearfully and wonderfully made, I am beautiful, I am a King's daughter – heiress to the throne – I have a purpose, I am loved unconditionally, I am equipped to win every battle, I have already won the war, I am healed. Through you, I am confident! I stand on your promises and receive everything you have for me. I am not afraid to win, and I am not afraid to proclaim where my victory comes from. You, oh God, have set me free. I thank you, I love you, I give you all the glory.

In the mighty and matchless name of
Jesus Christ,
Amen

Love, your daughter

Your signature _____

This book is devoted to the small voice in your spirit that speaks to the greater you.
You can and you will!
For my family — especially my mom, my bonus mom, my spiritual mom, and my sisters — and for my girlfriends, never stop fighting to become the woman God called you to be.
She's worth it!

I Am More Than Enough

*Not that we are sufficient of ourselves to think
any thing as of ourselves; but our sufficiency is
of God.*

2 Corinthians 3:5

When the waves of life hit, we're strong enough to withstand the first few. But then your legs may begin to quiver with fatigue, your shoulders begin to slump from your breathing no longer being controlled, and you find that the smallest wave knocks you flat on your back. As you lay there with each passing wave, large and small, smacking into you, you begin to feel that these are battles you cannot win, that you aren't equipped to win because you just aren't enough. You may think perhaps there is something inherently wrong with you and that's why you can't fight and win. But that's just it! There is nothing wrong with you, but you alone cannot fight and win. God's Word tells us that we are enough because of Him! You have to tap into the power and sufficiency of God to know your sufficiency is of Him! Sufficiency is your portion!

Dear Heavenly Father,

Thank you for choosing me and loving me first! Thank you for loving me unconditionally so that I am always connected to your power and sufficiency. Lord, help me to strengthen in my faith in you as I trust that I am enough because of you. I know there is nothing too big or too hard for you, so today I declare that I am yours, and I am sufficient!

In the mighty name of Jesus,
Amen

NOTES

Everything I Need Is Within Me

But if the Spirit of him that raised up Jesus from the dead dwell in you, he that raised up Christ from the dead shall also quicken your mortal bodies by his Spirit that dwelleth in you.

Romans 8:11

Every person is like an investment. God has deposited a lot into each of us, but instead of the market dictating the return, we do! Since God gave us much, much is required. Everything I do is because of Him. He put it in me and He is expecting a return, and I'm blessed to give it to Him! I am SO human! But I trust God to put HIS super on my natural, which produces what you call "superwoman." It's literally all God! He's placed on the inside of me to be wife, mother, minister, attorney, author, business owner, and who knows what else! Our job is simply to produce a return on His investment for His glory! Fulfillment is your portion!

Dear Heavenly Father,

I thank you for trusting me with purpose, gifts, anointing, strength, wisdom, and more in your name! Thank you for the power of the grave-conquering blood that covers me, my family, and every part of my life. Thank you for the gift of the Holy Spirit on the inside of me that I may have all that I may ever need. Cleanse me that I may be able to house your Holy Spirit. I release everything to you and submit my body, spirit, and life to you. Today, I will not worry about anything. With your grace and your guidance, I will do what I can and give to you what I can't. I trust you! I trust the power and the gifts that you've put within me. I trust that you will supply every need. Thank you, God! Thank you for power. Thank you for fulfillment. Thank you for allowing me to be complete in you.

In the mighty name of Jesus I pray,
Amen

NOTES

I Am Beautiful Just the Way I Am; There Are No Mistakes in Me

I will praise thee; for I am fearfully and wonderfully made: marvellous are thy works; and that my soul knoweth right well.

Psalm 139:14

Everywhere you look there is something telling you, subliminally, that you are not enough. Social media, TV, movies, music, and advertisements are all telling you that something needs to change – whether it's your weight, your body, your skin, parts of your face, your hair, and more! Sometimes we even see that there is something wrong with our personality because it doesn't "fit in" with the norms of society. Are you a woman who is assertive or a man who chooses when to exercise his words of wisdom? Society and the societal norms perpetuated by those around us can begin to wear us down and play on our self-confidence. But God said that you are made in HIS image and that HE cannot make a mistake. Have confidence in knowing that you were tailor-made by God himself, and His standards far surpass the world's. God's perfection is your portion!

Dear Heavenly Father,

Thank you for choosing me to be created, and for creating me in your perfect image! Help me to see myself the way you see me, loving every bit of myself both inside and out. I am encouraged to have the opportunity to grow to be more Christlike every day because I am your child. Let today be the first day of forever that I walk in confidence, knowing that I am beautiful just the way YOU created me.

In the mighty name of Jesus I pray,
Amen

NOTES

I Forgive Myself Because I Am Already Forgiven

To the praise of the glory of his grace, wherein he hath made us accepted in the beloved. In whom we have redemption through his blood, the forgiveness of sins, according to the riches of his grace.

Ephesians 1:6-7

Forgiveness, in itself, can be tough, but we know that it is a must. So we push past feelings of hurt, pain, and disappointment to forgive – sometimes even forgiving those who are not sorry. We are pursuing being Christlike, so we forgive and forgive and forgive. But what about us? We tend to forget about forgiving ourselves. We fall short of the glory at times, and we make mistakes, stumbling and falling. But God still forgives us, and he forgives us quickly at that! When things go wrong, how often do we replay that scenario in our heads over and over again?

Questioning what happened or wondering what we could have done differently. We hold it over ourselves far too long. The beauty of God is that He is not like us; He pours on His love and forgiveness thick, unconditionally. God already knew that we would fall short on our path to righteousness and yet He said that we are still worth it. He stayed on the cross for us, for times like this, for our eternal gift of life. Because of His sacrifice and love, we are already forgiven, so now it's time to forgive ourselves. Forgiveness is your portion!

Dear Heavenly Father,

I am not perfect, but you love me anyway. You look past my imperfections and choose to pour into me. Thank you for your forgiveness, restoring me each time I fall short. Your grace and mercy are unending, and I don't take that for granted. If you are able to love me past all of my imperfections and shortcomings, then I can surely do the same. Father, because you have shown me unconditional love and forgiveness, I can love and forgive myself too. I am worth it. You are not looking for perfection, you are looking for willingness, and Father, I am willing. For your glory, I am willing to release myself from the hurt, pain, and disappointment I hold against myself. You believe I am worth so much more! Because of you, I believe that too! I forgive myself, Father. Thank you and I love you.

In the mighty name of Jesus I pray,
Amen.

NOTES

I Am Stronger Than I Could Ever Imagine Because I Trust God

Then was the king exceedingly glad for him, and commanded that they should take Daniel up out of the den. So Daniel was taken up out of the den, and no manner of hurt was found upon him, because he believed in his God.

Daniel 6:23

Often times, we feel thrown and tossed about into situations that were strategically designed to make us feel discouraged and defeated. Again, it was designed to make you feel that way, but actually, it cannot make you feel that way. Why not? Because the enemy doesn't have that kind of power! Try as he may, he will never have the power to defeat you unless you give him that power. He has a way of making things seem so real! Yet after every triumph, we see just how far from the truth our situations were, just like Daniel. After being thrown into the lion's den, who wouldn't think that Daniel was faced with sudden death? But God! Even in the face of imminent death, Daniel trusted God for His truth to reveal itself. Daniel's belief saved him, just as yours will. Today, no matter what the enemy has crafted before your physical eyes, open up your spiritual eyes to God's truth and trust God! God's saving grace is your portion!

Dear Heavenly Father,

Thank you for being the truth. Create in me a spirit that is sensitive to your truth. I pray that you open up my spiritual eyes and my spiritual ears so that I am not discouraged or defeated by lies but strengthened and encouraged by your truth. Lord, I believe in you and you alone. No matter what I face in my day, I will trust in you. Today, I will shine your truth on the lies of my life, and I will walk in truth!

In the mighty name of Jesus I pray,
Amen.

NOTES

I Am Fearless Because I Am My Father's

*For God hath not given us the spirit of fear; but
of power, and of love, and of a sound mind.*

2 Timothy 1:7

The world can shy away from people who are
too bold, too confident, and too assertive in
themselves and in their walk for Christ. Trust
me, I know all about that. But how people
react to the boldness God has given you and
called for us all to have says more about them
than it does about you. Each one of us is made
in the image of God, the Almighty God!
That's a heavy cross to bear, but we bear it
with pride! We are His children; therefore,
we cannot have fear. Fear is a fruit of the
enemy. Just like the Bible says you will know
a tree by its fruit, the Lord knows if you are
His by the fruit you bear, and so does the
world. The world doesn't want you to be
fearless because it will cause them to be
uncomfortable. It causes them to have to look

at their own walk and see that God requires more. Never be afraid to give God more, because He multiplies everything we give to Him! If Jesus can feed thousands with two fish and five loaves of bread, imagine what He can do with your life! Be bold and give it all to God! Wear your crown proudly, Queen. Fearlessness is your portion!

Dear Heavenly Father,

I am your daughter, the daughter of a king. You are almighty, undefeated, undefeatable, all-knowing, and victorious. I am your heir and receive in the inheritance of your fearless power. Through you, I am undefeated and undefeatable. Through you, I am and will always be victorious. Thank you, Father, for choosing me and loving me. Thank you for allowing me to inherit all that you have for me. I have nothing to fear because I am yours. From this day forward, fear shall not be my portion! I will walk in power!

In the mighty name of Jesus I pray,
Amen

NOTES

I Am Complete

*I am the vine, ye are the branches: He that
abideth in me, and I in him, the same bringeth
forth much fruit: for without me ye can do
nothing.*

John 15:5

Situations in life have a tendency to rob you;
they steal your joy, your smile, your peace,
and your confidence. They come in and take
up space in your mind, paying rent with
misery. Soon, you may begin to feel like
you're losing touch with who you thought
you were, or who you thought you were
called to be. Soon, it seems like life is
withdrawing from you and nothing is
depositing, leaving you less than complete
and, in worse cases, completely empty. But
let me shed some truth on those withdrawals:
they're not your truth. They were designed to
look and feel real, but it's all a facade. They
seem so real because the enemy studies you

and knows exactly how to push buttons and pull heartstrings. He knows how to mess with your mind. But you have the power to cast out the darkness of his lies with the light of the truth, God's truth! The truth for your life is that God has equipped you with everything you need for every situation you face. The gift of the Holy Spirit is our eternal connection to the ultimate source, the ultimate truth. And with it, we have every deposit we could ever ask for and more! Completion is your portion!

Dear Heavenly Father,

Thank you for the gift of your truth and the filling of your Holy Spirit. Help me to allow your light to shine on every dark area in my life that seems to be robbing me of the things that come from you, Lord. My completion lies in you and in you alone, and no one has the power to take that away unless I let them. Thank you, Lord.

In Jesus name, I am complete!
Amen

NOTES

Blessings Are Already Mine

*And this is the confidence that we have in him,
that, if we ask anything according to his will, he
heareth us:*

1 John 5:14

Have you ever felt like nothing was working
out in your favor? Maybe you've put so much
energy and maybe even resources into
something and it still isn't working out. In
your mind and in your heart, you may believe
that what you are putting your energy into is
exactly what you need. But have you stopped
to see if that is what God wants for you? The
reason it's not working out is that it isn't
God's will for your life. In fact, He has
something better in store! You've heard it
before – God is in the blessing business. But
be advised, He is not in the forcing business.
The Lord will never force you to accept what
He has for you; you always have a choice. He
wants to bless you. In fact, there are already

blessings with your name on it! It's up to you to receive them. Today, submit your plans, goals, and works unto the Lord and see what blessings He has for you! Blessings are your portion!

Dear Heavenly Father,

Thank you for loving me in such a way that you want to bless me. Today, Lord, I submit to you my plans, my goals, and works! I want your will to be done in my life, for your glory. Father, I know that greater is you and that your plans are far better than anything I could ever hope or wish for, so I say YES! – yes to your plans for my life and yes to your way. Humbly I kneel before you to receive every blessing with my name on it.

In the mighty name of Jesus,
Amen

NOTES

I'm Not Just Called – I'm Chosen

For many are called, but few are chosen.

Matthew 22:14

It's true, Christ died for all. He died for the holier-than-thou and the sinner, the healer and the drug addict, the straight-and-narrow and the "I'll try anything once." Yes, there is nothing that separates you from the love of God. But there are levels to this thing. Don't believe me? Check out our Scripture focus. In this text, Jesus is giving a parable of what the kingdom of heaven is like, comparing it to a wedding that is to take place where many are invited but still, someone showed up improperly dressed. Naturally, he could not come in to the wedding. We are cordially invited to be a part of the kingdom agenda. There is no limitation on who can get the invitation, but we have to dress the part. The amazing thing about this is that you already have everything you need in order to be the part. You are a descendant of the King who's giving the invitations. It's natural. As a matter of fact, it's supernatural. Daughter, walk in His likeness because you are already chosen – It's time to walk like it!

Dear Heavenly Father,

Thank you for being so gracious and merciful in choosing me to be a part of the kingdom. Thank you for calling me and choosing me. Fix my posture to walk more like you, shift my language to talk more like you, change my heart to love and forgive like you. I bless your name and thank you for not only calling me but choosing me. Because of your grace and mercy, unconditional love, and unconditional forgiveness, I am chosen! Thank you, Father.

In the mighty name of Jesus,
Amen

NOTES

In the Name of Jesus, Today Is a Blessing!

Blessed is the man that trusteth in the Lord, and whose hope the Lord is.

Jeremiah 17:7

It's easy to get caught up in the day-to-day. "Wash, rinse, repeat." It's time to change that mentality! Every day is a gift! It sounds cliché but truly, someone did not wake up this morning. Someone woke up with a loss function in their mind, their limbs, their hearing, or even their eyesight! I knew a young man who had an accident at the age of 27 and lost everything but his life. He is now mentally challenged. He can't walk or talk, and he can't take care of himself. He had just had a daughter and had his entire life before him. In an instant, it was gone. We have so much to be grateful for! And we know that we have the power to speak life! Your reality is a manifestation of the thoughts, words, and actions you have released and believed. Take inventory of your mind and heart today. Figure out what needs to go and start speaking those things as if they were so. Speak it until you believe because, as the Bible says, if you believe it and receive, then it is yours. Today will be whatever you make it. Make today a blessing!

Dear Heavenly Father,

You are so amazing for smiling down on me and putting me on the wake-up list! Your grace and mercies overflow in my life as I have the opportunity to do what you have called me to do. I bless and worship your name because you are more than deserving. Father, be with me in everything I do, everything I put my hands to, and every door I walk through. You are the Author and Finisher of my faith and, Lord, I have faith and speak that today is a blessing! Today is a blessing from you and I couldn't ask for anything more. Thank you, Jesus.

In the mighty name of Jesus,
Amen

NOTES

I Am Anointed to Walk Through Every Door God Guides Me To

For we are his workmanship, created in Christ Jesus unto good works, which God hath before ordained that we should walk in them.
Ephesians 2:10

There are 7.7 billion people, and counting, on earth, yet the Bible says repeatedly that all have been called for the glorification of the kingdom. The kingdom made an investment when God sent His only son to bear the weight of sin for all sinners; Christ died for every one of us, not just some. And each of us has the ability to receive eternal life and life more abundantly. Each person has a purpose, and all they have to do is accept it. Isn't that amazing? 7.7 billion people and God has a purpose for them all, if they so choose! Finding yourself in situations where you don't feel qualified is a sign that God is in the midst. It's not about whether you are qualified because in all honesty, we're not, but when God is in control, He provides the grace and anointing to do that which He is calling you to. You are in that place for a reason. God needs kingdom people like you walking through the right doors, sitting at the right tables, touching the right people. The kingdom agenda goes beyond the church walls and mission trips. The light, love, and truth of Christ is needed everywhere. So as you walk through those doors and sit at those tables and have those conversations, know that God has already provided the anointing and grace required. Stand tall and have Godfidence!

Dear Heavenly Father,

Thank you for your trust in me, that I may do what you have called me to do. Father, remove fear and doubt in me, that I may have Godfidence, knowing that I am meant to be exactly where you've placed me. I am equipped with the anointing and grace to carry out your kingdom agenda for your glory and for the edification of the body of Christ. Today, and every day, I shift my posture to exude an attitude of confidence and humility. I am yours and I am called according to your purpose because I have chosen you back and I love you. In Jesus' name, I am fully equipped!

In the mighty name of Jesus,
Amen

NOTES

I May Not Have Everything I Want, but I Have Everything I Need

But my God shall supply all your need according to his riches in glory by Christ Jesus.

Philippians 4:19

It is so easy to get bogged down with the things that we want, or at least what we think we want. Whatever you focus on gets bigger, so the more you focus on what you want, the bigger your seeming lack becomes. Instead of focusing on what you don't have, use the notes section today to write down everything you do have. Make a complete list of everything and focus on those things, revisiting this page often. You can start your list with things that seem simple to you, the things we tend to take for granted like waking up this morning, then go as deep as you're led. Thank God for these things, because it could've been another story. God is your total supply and having every need met is your portion!

Dear Heavenly Father,

Today, I shift my heart from a place of wanting to a place of gratitude. God, I thank you for life and life more abundantly. Thank you for your sacrifice on the cross. Thank you for blessing me with brand new mercies every morning. Thank you for your love, grace, mercy, and forgiveness. Thank you for the people you've placed in my life and the people you've removed. Thank you for loving me enough to allow me to go through trials so that I may be perfected for this kingdom work. In every situation, you've sustained me and have never forsaken me. I have you and because of this, I have everything I need, and I am forever grateful. Thank you, God!

In the mighty name of Jesus,
Amen

NOTES

I Am Chosen

*But ye are a chosen generation, a royal
priesthood, an holy nation, a peculiar people;
that ye should shew forth the praises of him who
hath called you out of darkness into his
marvellous light;*

1 Peter 2:9

Every day you wake up, you have choices to
make. Some may not feel like a choice, but
you always have a choice. Particularly, you
have a choice in whether or not you will be
obedient to Christ. He has called you to be
great and an integral part of the kingdom
work, but will you listen to Him? Will you
surrender your will to Him and do His will
for your life, knowing that His will is perfect?
Many of us struggle with laying our will
down at God's feet for various reasons, but
they all boil down to fear and lack of trust.
Can you imagine if Jesus thought like us? In
Luke 22:42, Jesus asked for this cup to be

removed from Him, cup meaning His assignment to be crucified. But He completed His request by saying, "Nevertheless not my will, but thine, be done." Jesus was then strengthened by an angel and continued on to complete the assignment. Jesus chose to obey His Father's will for the sake of you and me! He had the hardest assignment anyone could ever have, and He said yes! You are not here by coincidence. Your life was ordained a long time ago, as you were chosen to be a part of the greatest gift on earth and in heaven. You are chosen, Queen!

Dear Heavenly Father,

Thank you for choosing me. Thank you for submitting your will to the Father so that I may have life and life more abundantly through your sacrifice. You had the power to get off of the cross, but you stayed on for me! I can never repay you. All I have is my life. Just as you have chosen me, I choose you. I submit my will to you, and I say yes. I am your heiress, a part of the royal priesthood and chosen for this generation. Father, I say yes! I choose you.

In the mighty name of Jesus,
Amen

NOTES

I Have the Power to Choose Life

*And I give unto them eternal life; and they shall
never perish, neither shall any man pluck them
out of my hand.*

John 10:28

The first time I read this verse, I was
immediately floored! We always hear about
the eternal life we've been gifted but never
the fact that no one can snatch us out of the
hand of God. It got me thinking because there
are times when we are not in God's hand and
are out of the will of God. How does that
happen? If no one can snatch us from the
hand of God, that means we walk out of the
hand of God. Yikes! I'm sure it's not our
intention, but it happens. But the beauty of
the Almighty is that we have the power, just
as we walked out, to walk right back in! You
have the power to choose eternal life in the
hand of God! This is the greatest power we
have. God is powerful enough to ensure that

no one can snatch you from His hand, but also so understanding (and forgiving) when we walk out of His hand. Because of the power given to us, we can return home; we can choose life with the Father! There is nothing too big or too messy for God to forgive and fix, but it starts with you choosing life. Life is your portion!

Dear Heavenly Father,

My God! Thank you for life. Thank you for exercising your almighty power to keep me from being snatched out of your hand. Father, strengthen me to remain steadfast in you, and never walking out of your hand. Cover my mind, protect my heart, and strengthen the Spirit within me, the Holy Spirit, to remain in your will at all times, surrendering my will to you. Today, I make the vow to walk back into your hands and remain there. Thank you for receiving me.

In the mighty name of Jesus,
Amen

NOTES

I Am Healed Through Forgiveness

Let all bitterness, and wrath, and anger, and clamour, and evil speaking, be put away from you, with all malice: And be ye kind one to another, tenderhearted, forgiving one another, even as God for Christ's sake hath forgiven you.

Ephesians 4:31-32

Forgiveness isn't ignoring how you feel, because what you feel is real. The things that caused hurt, pain, and disappointment are real. Still, we must choose to forgive because forgiveness is for you and not for them. It is so that you can be free from the chains of pain and released from the mental prison of hurt and disappointment. So, we forgive them. I'll be the first to tell you how I used to suffer from unforgiveness. I thought there was strength in holding on to the hurt, and somehow the fact that I would not forgive the other person hurt them. These are lies that the enemy wants you to believe. Unforgiveness is comfortable because it gives you control. You were unable to control the other person and often times, the situation blindsided you. So the only way to gain control of the situation is to hold on to the pain. Of course, you're not holding on to the pain intentionally, but it is how we are wired. It is human nature to need control. But what is more powerful is releasing that false sense of power and laying it at the feet of Jesus. Jesus is the ultimate healer and deliverer. He is the only one who can cleanse, restore, and make whole. It's a matter of whether you trust God to do the work only He can do. Trust me, unforgiveness does nothing good for you or the situation. In fact, the Bible says to forgive so that you can also be forgiven. After all, we are human too. God has given us wisdom and guidance to not remain in abusive situations or return to the fire He just delivered us from, but for His glory, we have to forgive. Your healing begins when you forgive. Allow God to cover you in love, strengthen you with grace, and deal with your situation in a way you could have never imagined. All you need to do is forgive and walk in God. Healing through forgiveness is your portion.

Dear Heavenly Father,

Blessed be your name for delivering me from this pain, hurt, and disappointment. Thank you for giving me the strength to forgive. I am humble enough to know that there are times when I need forgiveness too, so I give it freely so that you can forgive me freely. As you deliver me from my situation and make a way out of no way, I keep my eyes focused steadfastly on you. My feet are planted in love and righteousness. I trust you, Father. Because of my obedience, I forgive and I am healed. Through your Word and our relationship, I am given guidance and wisdom. Your divine will shall be done, and I will no longer be a prisoner of unforgiveness. I am free! Thank you, Lord.

In the mighty name of Jesus,
Amen

NOTES

I Am Prosperous

Beloved, I wish above all things that thou mayest prosper and be in health, even as thy soul prospereth.

3 John 1:2

Such sweet words! But more than words, they are a prayer for these things concerning your life. I never shy away from the belief that we were created to be healthy, wealthy, and prosperous. It says it in the Bible! Don't let anyone make you feel bad for wanting or having good health, wealth, and prosperity. You are a kingdom child – what else is an heiress supposed to have? I'm not sure where the culture of shame came in wanting more for ourselves, but do not let that be your portion. You were created by the King of kings, Lord of lords. Even if you do not yet have your prosperity, it's only a matter of time because it's already yours! Don't be concerned with what your present situation looks like. Trust your Father to deliver exactly what you've been promised – prosperity in all things and in your health, as your soul prospers. There's not much else to say; prosperity is your portion.

Dear Heavenly Father,

Gracious, sweet, and kind Father, thank you for making all my ways prosperous. I stand firm in the belief and knowledge that this is so for my life because I am your daughter. Nothing shall change my mind, and I speak it daily. I am healthy, wealthy, and prosperous, according to your will for my life, and I thank you.

In the mighty name of Jesus,
Amen

NOTES

The Lord Knows the Deepest Desires of My Heart and Will Fulfill Them

Delight thyself also in the LORD; and he shall give thee the desires of thine heart.

Psalm 37:4

God knows your heart and knows the love you have for Him. His love, grace, and mercy know no end. His power and ability we can never fathom. When God works things out, He does so in a way that we could have never done ourselves or even begin to formulate. He is so almighty! That same power that makes a way out of no way is the same power that knows your heart's deepest desires and will fulfill them according to His perfect plan for your life. There is nothing wrong with having desire, such as to be a wife, have children, become wealthy, preach and prophesy, and more. God places these desires in our hearts in order to fulfill the kingdom's agenda and to fulfill you. Your completion will always come through Christ, so know and trust that just as with everything else in your life, He is working out your desires as well. Your heart's desires are important to the kingdom. The fulfillment of your deepest desires is your portion!

Dear Heavenly Father,

You know the depths of my mind, heart, and soul. I lay every desire at your feet and give you thanks in advance for fulfilling them in a way only you can, for your glory. I trust you, God. I trust your will for my life, I trust your way for my life, I trust your timing. Thank you for being the God who cares about everything concerning me, big and small. I bless your name and give you all the glory.

In Jesus' mighty name,
Amen

NOTES

Everything I Put My Hands to Prospers

*Thou shalt surely give him, and thine heart shall
not be grieved when thou givest unto him,
because for this thing the Lord thy God shall
bless thee in all thy works and in all that thou
puttest thine hand unto;*

Deuteronomy 15:10

It is so amazing how God can see the very
depths of our hearts. He knows that we have
a heart to love, to give, and to do, but
sometimes we second-guess our givings and
our doings. Are we giving in vain? Are we
spinning our wheels trying to make this thing
work? Should we even be going after this?
When it comes to God-ordained assignments,
trust and believe there are also tools of the
enemy on assignment as well. So when you
find yourself asking these questions or
feeling discouragement in any form, know
that your works are already blessed! It says it
right here in his Word. When you put your

hands to the works God has called you to, sit back and relax, knowing that all your works are being blessed.

Dear Heavenly Father,

Thank you for trusting me with assignments for the kingdom, and for blessing them. I thank you for allowing my life to be fulfilled with you, and for my works to be covered and protected by you always. Father, I thank you for allowing me to prosper in all that I put my hands to. Thank you for prospering my joy, my mind, my health, my family, my finances, my present, and my future. With you, I cannot and will not fail. All things will be blessed. Thank you for being so gracious, Father. I love you.

In the mighty name of Jesus I pray,
Amen

NOTES

I Can Stand Tall and Strong Before Anyone Because I Kneel Before the Lord of Lords

That at the name of Jesus every knee should bow, of things in heaven, and things in earth, and things under the earth;

Philippians 2:10

You are blessed, loved, and favored. Walking in your purpose and submitting to God, you are bound to meet some adversity. Why? Well, naturally, the enemy doesn't want you to thwart his plans. He works day and night, building and utilizing his army against the kingdom and its people. So, naturally, as a kingdom daughter, you will be attacked. Remain diligent and cognizant of the fact that the enemy will use any and everything to attack you. The people closest to you and the most sacred areas of your life are not exempt. As the enemy prowls and attacks, he doesn't tire like you might; he is consistently persistent. That is why prayer is non-negotiable. Yes, the enemy is a defeated foe but only when we are in battle the right way. The Bible says in Ephesians 6:12–13: "For we wrestle not against flesh and blood, but against principalities, against powers, against the rulers of the darkness of this world, against spiritual wickedness in high places. Wherefore take unto you the whole armor of God, that ye may be able to withstand in the evil day, and having done all, to stand." Therefore, you fight and win battles on your knees, in prayer, praying always in the Holy Spirit. When you kneel before God and allow your battles to be won through Him, you can stand tall against any adversary, even the ones that sting the most. Victory is your portion!

Dear Heavenly Father,

You are almighty, unchanging, and never failing. Thank you for allowing the power and victory of the Holy Spirit to be within me. Through you, I am able to win every battle. Through prayer in your Son's name, I am victorious. Father, give me a heart and mind to pray always. Strengthen my heart and mind to withstand the attacks. Focus my discernment, that I may see the enemy clearly. In every battle, keep me and guide me, that I may always remain in your will, coming out victorious. Thank you for the victory.

In the mighty name of Jesus,
Amen

NOTES

_____

_____

_____

_____

_____

_____

_____

_____

_____

No Matter What It Looks Like, Everything Is Working Out for My Good

Being confident of this very thing, that he which hath begun a good work in you will perform it until the day of Jesus Christ:

Philippians 1:6

Frustratingly exhales

The enemy has such a way of painting these false pictures in our lives that look so real. He takes real facts and puts them together in a way that looks so true! But thank God facts do not equate truth! We must seek God in everything we go through. What is God saying about the situation? Where is God in the situation? Does God have a purpose for this? Is this God or is this the enemy? It takes a mature heart to not react to everything thrown our way, but to take the time to step back and really assess what is before us. Many times, we'll find that things are quite as they seem. Sometimes an attack is not an attack but a lesson for growth. Sometimes a person is not trying to hurt you, but their words came out wrong. Other times, a situation looks like it's not God's will but God is waiting to take control so He can blow your mind with His will in His way. When things are going haywire and you're struggling to see God in it, take a step back and seek truth; seek God. He will reveal His truth and work it all out for your good. It's His work, and His name is on it. It will not fail! YOU WILL NOT FAIL! Hold tight, sis. Failure is not your portion!

Dear Heavenly Father,

Thank you for your unwavering commitment to the work you've put on the inside of me. Doubt is removed from me as I trust that this work you have begun in me will be completed. I hold steadfastly onto your truth so that I am not discouraged by the false pictures of the enemy. Facts are not truth, and I will see your truth in all things. Thank you for clarity, thank you for strength, thank you for victory. I shall not fail.

In the mighty name of Jesus I pray,
Amen

NOTES

I Will Conquer Every Challenge That Comes My Way

Nay, in all these things we are more than conquerors through him that loved us.

Romans 8:37

Ready or not, challenges are headed your way (if they're not already here). The Bible says that weapons formed against us shall not prosper, not that they won't form. Challenges are inevitable. It's not a matter of if challenges will come, but what will you do when they do. Much like our humanistic responses, you have two ways you can react: you can run or you can fight. Although running may be a natural response to challenges, I assure you it is the wrong response. Why? Because there is no logic in running from a challenge you've already conquered. When you are in God, you are more than a conqueror through Him. Earlier, you learned that the right way to fight your battles is on your knees. Challenges are no different. God is the orchestrator of our lives, and His plan is perfect. Knowing that we are already victorious, fight! Be encouraged to get into your closet and pray. Pray from your heart, being vulnerable with your Father. It doesn't have to be anything fancy. Bring to him your challenges and position your mind, knowing that you have already conquered them. Conquering challenges is your portion!

Dear Heavenly Father,

I stand on your Word. Boldly I proclaim that I am a conqueror. There is no challenge that can overtake me, there is nothing too big or too hard for you. I cast aside all fear and doubt, knowing that I am yours and you love me. It is in this love that I receive your promises. In you, I am a conqueror. Thank you, Jesus. I love you.

In the mighty name of Jesus,
Amen

NOTES

I Have the Power to Change My Situation by Shifting My Mindset

Jesus answered and said unto them, Verily I say unto you, If ye have faith, and doubt not, ye shall not only do this which is done to the fig tree, but also if ye shall say unto this mountain, Be thou removed, and be thou cast into the sea; it shall be done. And all things, whatsoever ye shall ask in prayer, believing, ye shall receive.

Matthew 21:21–22

You may be going through something that feels like no matter your efforts, it's not moving. You've prayed, fasted, and sought wise counsel. Why is nothing happening? It's time to evaluate your level of faith. The Bible says that we have the power to move a mountain into the sea! If we can do that, then surely we can shift this situation of ours. All we need is faith. Search yourself. Are you really walking in true faith or are you just hoping for something to happen? There is nothing wrong with hope, but in order to shift this thing, you have to step your faith up to 1000! Speak as if it is already so. Proclaim what you want to be true often. Write down your proclamations. Your situation will have no choice but to submit to the power of your words because you are operating in complete faith. Ask for it in prayer and believe it is already done. Not that it might be done or that you hope it will be done. IT.IS.DONE. Faith is your portion!

*For today, write in your personal prayer, using full faith and believing that it is already received.

_____

_____

_____

_____

_____

_____

_____

NOTES

_____

_____

_____

_____

_____

_____

_____

_____

_____

_____

_____

_____

_____

_____

_____

_____

_____

_____

I Have Nothing to Worry About – the Lord Hears My Every Cry

In my distress I called upon the Lord, and cried unto my God: he heard my voice out of his temple, and my cry came before him, even into his ears.

Psalm 18:6

It's so amazing that the Almighty God, who created the heavens and the earth, has the heart to take the time to hear our cries. How awesome is that? You are never alone. Even when you are going through and it feels that you are, you're not. Everything you go through and every tear that falls, God sees it all, and He is right there with you. Your tears and sorrow are only for a moment, and what is to come is greater than anything you could ever imagine! God does not like to see you suffer, so know that the sufferings of this present time are not worthy to be compared with the glory which shall be revealed in us (Romans 8:18). That means none of this is in vain; God will use all of this for your good, and everything the enemy meant for evil will be used for your benefit. And just imagine, the same God who intricately designed the heavens and the earth is working on your situation right now! The same God! Settle your spirit and rest your mind; you can dry your tears because it is already taken care of.

Dear Heavenly Father,

I come to you baring all. You know every corner of me, and I have nothing to hide. My mind is cluttered, my heart is heavy, and my tears are many. Still, I know that there's nothing too big for you. My problems that seem like giants are but ants to you. I relinquish my worries to you, Father, taking your yoke because it's light. I lay everything at your feet and know that you hear my every cry. Thank you for being a present God, and

I thank you for taking care of this, and everything, for me. I give you all the glory.

In the mighty name of Jesus,
Amen

NOTES

I Am Deserving of Every Good Thing God Has For Me

*For the Lord God is a sun and shield:
the Lord will give grace and glory: no good
thing will he withhold from them that walk
uprightly.*

Psalm 84:11

Today is a day of affirmations. Today, you will walk boldly, proudly, and confidently in who you are because you know whose you are. You have a beautiful heart. Your spirit attracts the things and the people that line up with your destiny. You are in your right mind. God has ordered your steps and your walk into your purpose. You receive every blessing and every promise God has for you. You are worthy of God's best. You are deserving of every good thing God has for you. You will receive everything God has for you. What are some affirmations you hear

God telling you? Write them in the notes section.

Dear Heavenly Father,

I am yours. You are the Almighty Father whose love and grace know no end, and your blessings are tailor-made for me. What you are about to do in my life, no ear has heard and no eye has seen. God, I receive it all right now! I cannot thank you enough and worship you enough for keeping me in your hand, covering me and loving me. Lord, I glorify your name and marvel at your works. Truly, you are the Great I Am, the Messiah. I am forever humbled and grateful that you would choose me to receive your inheritance. I bless you, God.

In the mighty name of Jesus,
Amen

NOTES

My Work Is Not in Vain

I the Lord search the heart, I try the reins, even to give every man according to his ways, and according to the fruit of his doings.

Jeremiah 17:10

They say an overnight success takes 10 years. 10 years! How long have you been working at your craft? Don't be discouraged or deflated when you feel like things aren't moving. Entrepreneurs often say they were just grinding, day in and day out, doing what they knew needed to be done, and then one day they looked up and saw the empire they built. They weren't focused on what was or wasn't, they were focused on what's to come. In their hearts, they knew success was theirs and they just had to keep going in the right direction, no matter how long it took. What they saw in the end was the fruit of their doings. Because you are a child of God, you have the opportunity to receive even more over your works according to today's Scripture. Each day, you are working diligently, keeping God at the forefront, operating in truth and love. Allow God to be your guide in all things. Your work may be a business, or it may be ministry, school, family, work, or something unique God has assigned to you. In all of it, keep your heart pure and focused on God, be truthful and loving in all your ways, and work to produce fruits that glorify God. God's blessings shall be plentiful and your works shall be rewarded. Meaningful work is your portion!

Dear Heavenly Father,

You are so gracious to look down upon me and see my works. Lord, you see my labor and you know my heart. If there be anything that is not of you in my heart, cleanse me now so that I may receive all that you have for me. Please bless my works so that I may have increase and live life more abundantly as you have called me to. Father, I stand on your word and know that you are a just God.

Search my heart, try the reins, and bless me according to your measure. I thank you for increase and overflow in my works.

In the mighty name of Jesus I pray,
Amen

NOTES

God Has More and Better in Store for Me

Though thy beginning was small, yet thy latter end should greatly increase.

Job 8:7

Beginnings can be tough and, at times, discouraging. New jobs, new relationships, new babies, new businesses, a new walk in God, and the like are examples. All of these can be very exciting but also very difficult to navigate, initially. A lot of times, we have an idea of what we want things to look like, how we feel they should be, and have our own timing. But, as the saying goes, we are not in control. And that's okay! In fact, you should prefer it that way because God is in complete control. When it comes to what God has called you to do, it can be especially difficult or frustrating and may not look like God in the beginning. There may even be people who try to discourage you from what God has called you to. But don't allow it! God's unique purpose in your life is meant to be effective, life-changing, and lifelong. Those things cannot be achieved overnight. Take a look at Rome, the Sistine Chapel ceiling, Amazon, Microsoft, and even an apple tree. All of these things that we have come to love and enjoy today, things that have changed our very existence, took time and had to increase greatly over time. God sees you as more valuable than all of those things. So it's no wonder our beginning is small and things are not moving as fast as we'd like. It's because if God builds us too quickly, we won't be stable and we'll fall. Our foundation has to be sturdy so that our final production will last a lifetime. Find solace in knowing that this is just the beginning and greater is coming in His perfect timing. Increase is your portion!

Dear Heavenly Father,

Forgive my impatience and lack of understanding your will and your way for my life. I rejoice in knowing the truth, that I am your greatest work and you will not let me fail. Father, I thank you for taking the necessary time to make me great, to increase me! Although my beginning is small, I am grateful for a solid foundation being built, knowing that what's to come is greater than I could ever imagine. Thank you, Jesus, for loving me so! Your love comforts me as I wait, and your unfathomable artistry gives me confidence. You are so magnificent. Thank you, Lord!

In the mighty name of Jesus I pray,
Amen

NOTES

I Am Made in His Image, and I Won't Quit Because He Didn't

When Jesus therefore had received the vinegar, he said, It is finished: and he bowed his head, and gave up the ghost.

John 19:30

It is far too easy to complain. I'm no psychologist, but I'd argue that humans innately need and seek control. When things are beyond our control, we make rash decisions, like quitting. We have an idea of what we want certain things to look like or how they should turn out, and when they don't work out that way, some of us give up. It's not uncommon. But aren't you curious to know what would happen if you didn't quit? If you pushed past the stage of discomfort and disappointment, what could happen? If you got to the place where you could do nothing but leave it in God's hands, how would it turn out? Take Jesus as your example. When He was in the garden before the crucifixion, He wanted to quit, but He pushed through, obeying the Father's will. From there, the whole world was saved. Every single person is given the opportunity of eternal life because He didn't quit. That is your Father! If He didn't quit, neither should you. Completion is your portion!

Dear Heavenly Father,

Strengthen me in the way that you were strengthened in order to carry out your assignment. Help me, God, to never quit on the will you have for my life. I believe that what you have for me is the best for me, so I commit to finishing the race strong. Father, for your will and not mine, I will not quit. I know you have called me to be great and there are people who need what you've placed inside of me. So, for your glory, strengthen me. I thank you, Lord.

In the mighty name of Jesus,
Amen

NOTES

With God, I Can't Fail

*I can do all things through Christ which
strengtheneth me.*

Philippians 4:13

It's so cliché, I know. But truly, anything God
has called you to can be done through Him.
The awesome thing about God is that His
divine methods are unmatched. He has the
ability to create a way out of no way, in a way
that our minds cannot even conceptualize.
God will use anything to bring you through
for His glory. We can see the evidence of His
workmanship all around us. The method in
which we are able to breathe both
scientifically and medically, our entire
ecosystem, and the consistency and power of
the sunrise and sunset are all examples of the
intricate details and unfathomable ability of
our God. This same God is the one bringing
you through to your destiny. Destiny is a
journey, not a destination. It will take

supernatural strength to make it on this journey, but thankfully, you've got Christ. Failure is not your portion!

Dear Heavenly Father,

Thank you for success. As I walk in my purpose, I know that I will make it through this journey gracefully because I am walking through you. You have never failed me, God, and I know you never will. Thank you for being the true and living God that I can call upon and stand firmly on. Your truth and strength are unwavering, and you are so awesome. I marvel at your works. Thank you, oh God, for allowing me to do all things through you. Thank you for supernatural strength.

It is in the mighty name of Jesus I pray,
Amen

NOTES

Nothing Can Separate Me From God's Love

Who shall separate us from the love of Christ? shall tribulation, or distress, or persecution, or famine, or nakedness, or peril, or sword?

For I am persuaded, that neither death, nor life, nor angels, nor principalities, nor powers, nor things present, nor things to come, Nor height, nor depth, nor any other creature, shall be able to separate us from the love of God, which is in Christ Jesus our Lord.

Romans 8:35, 38–39

The grace of God was created for you, for all of us. It's frustrating when leaders chastise and rebuke without grace because that's simply not God. When Christ died on the cross, He died for all of us. When He rose after the third day, the deal was sealed and we were all given the gift of eternal life. Jesus stayed on the cross, knowing that He was dying for sinners who would stumble and fall, yet He stayed. We are encouraged to live according to the Word of God, walking upright in righteousness. And when we fall short, we repent and God is still close. When you begin to go through the hardest times of your life, you need to be reminded that there is nothing that can remove God from your life. If He didn't walk away from the cross, He certainly will not walk away from you in your situations. God is ever present. In every battle, every attack, every sin, and every situation, God's love abounds. Truly, it is unconditional. Never feel ashamed or so overwhelmed that you believe the enemy's lie that God and His love are absent. Stand on the Word of God; nothing will separate you from the love of God. Unconditional love is your portion!

Dear Heavenly Father,

Thank you for being ever present in my life and loving me unconditionally. I could not imagine my life without you and, thankfully, I never will. Father, as I go through pitfalls, attacks, battles, and more, help me to always remember that you are by my side and you will not remove your love from me. As you remain steadfast with me, I will also remain steadfast and I will not move from you. In you, I have unconditional love and I thank you.

In the mighty name of Jesus,
Amen

NOTES

Every Promise Will Come to Pass
Because God's Name Is on It

The Lord will perfect that which concerneth me:
thy mercy, O Lord, endureth forever: forsake not
the works of thine own hands.

Psalm 138:8

It is my prayer on this 30th day that you've grown closer to God and your confidence has increased exponentially, knowing that you are His beloved prized possession. His love for you knows no end, His forgiveness is abounding, and His grace and mercies are freely given. God has placed something amazing on the inside of you. There is no one like you! No one can fulfill your purpose here on this earth the way you can. In fact, your purpose is completely unique, and you are the only one who can do it. As these 30 days are closed out, know that the journey does not stop here. God is forever with you and will ensure that every promise will come to pass.

God cannot tell a lie and His name is on you. Trust Him in all your ways and watch the blessings flow. Today, and forevermore, I speak uncommon favor over your life and all that you put your hands to. I touch and agree with you that every promise over your life will come to pass and the enemy will get no victory. God will continue to give you the strength you need concerning the assignments He has given you. Remain confident in yourself through Christ, leaning on Him for everything. You are loved way more than you'll ever know. You are cherished and you are chosen. Confidence is your portion!

Dear Heavenly Father,

You are so worthy of all the glory and all the praise. You are a healer, a deliverer, a way maker, and a promise keeper. Through you, I am made whole. I know that I belong to you and I have a divine, unique purpose in the kingdom. Thank you for the confidence you've given me to be me, to be full of joy, and to walk in my purpose with my head held high, knowing that I am chosen. I give you my life and I submit my will to you. I trust the covering you have over my mind, heart, and soul. Today, and forevermore, I worship you, giving you all the glory for every blessing. In you and through you, I am a new creation: a confident woman of God. Thank you, Jesus! I love you.

In the mighty name of Jesus I pray,
Amen

NOTES

10 Days of Journaling
What Is God Saying to You?

DAY 31

Proverbs 3:5–6, Romans 12:2

NOTES

_____

_____

_____

_____

_____

_____

_____

_____

_____

_____

_____

_____

_____

_____

DAY 32

John 13:7

NOTES

_____

_____

_____

_____

_____

_____

_____

_____

_____

_____

_____

_____

_____

_____

Proverbs 3:26

NOTES

_____

_____

_____

_____

_____

_____

_____

_____

_____

_____

_____

_____

_____

_____

_____

1 Peter 5:7

NOTES

_____

_____

_____

_____

_____

_____

_____

_____

_____

_____

_____

_____

_____

_____

_____

_____

DAY 35

Deuteronomy 31:6

NOTES

_____

_____

_____

_____

_____

_____

_____

_____

_____

_____

_____

_____

_____

_____

DAY 36

Psalm 34:1

NOTES

_____

_____

_____

_____

_____

_____

_____

_____

_____

_____

_____

_____

_____

_____

Philippians 3:3

NOTES

_____

_____

_____

_____

_____

_____

_____

_____

_____

_____

_____

_____

_____

_____

DAY 38

2 Chronicles 32:8

NOTES

_____

_____

_____

_____

_____

_____

_____

_____

_____

_____

_____

_____

_____

_____

Proverbs 3:5

NOTES

_____

_____

_____

_____

_____

_____

_____

_____

_____

_____

_____

_____

_____

_____

_____

Jude 1:24

NOTES

_____

_____

_____

_____

_____

_____

_____

_____

_____

_____

_____

_____

_____

_____

_____

_____

_____

Over the past 40 days, you've laughed, cried, nodded in agreement, shouted out loud, and sighed, but most importantly, you've changed. You've grown closer to God, and so your walk is different and your talk is different. Your confidence is rooted in Christ, so now it's bold, unmovable, and unshakeable! That crown looks good on you, Queen.

Share this book with a woman you love

Find me online

Facebook.com/MrsCynthiaCFarmer
Instagram.com/cynthiacfarmer
Linkedin.com/in/ccfarmeresq

Feedback?

Email me at cynthiacfarmer@gmail.com

Speaking Requests

For speaking inquiries, please email
booking.cynthiacfarmer@gmail.com

About the Author

Cynthia C. Farmer was born in Brooklyn, New York and raised in Silver Spring, Maryland. Born to Haitian immigrants, she is a first-generation American and is one of four girls. Currently, Cynthia resides in Maryland with her husband, Isaac, and their three sons, Christian, Elijah, and Josiah. Professionally, Cynthia is an attorney and runs a boutique law firm. In ministry, she is an Elder and preacher in her church. Having gone through many trials as an African American woman in America, a single mom and then to a bonus mom, a wife, law school and then studying for the bar just four days after giving birth, and especially ministry with the enemy trying to silence her voice throughout her entire life, she has had to learn to root her confidence in God or otherwise be tossed around with the waves of life. *Confidence Is My Portion* is her debut devotional.

Made in the USA
Middletown, DE
26 March 2019